ABANDONED
FLINT

KYLE BROOKY

AMERICA
THROUGH TIME®
ADDING COLOR TO AMERICAN HISTORY

America Through Time is an imprint of Fonthill Media LLC
www.through-time.com
office@through-time.com

Published by Arcadia Publishing by arrangement with Fonthill Media LLC
For all general information, please contact Arcadia Publishing:
Telephone: 843-853-2070
Fax: 843-853-0044
E-mail: sales@arcadiapublishing.com
For customer service and orders:
Toll-Free 1-888-313-2665

www.arcadiapublishing.com

First published 2020

ISBN 978-1-63499-208-4

Typeset in Trade Gothic 10pt on 15pt
Printed and bound in England

CONTENTS

ABOUT THE AUTHOR

KYLE BROOKY has always been interested in the strange and offbeat. From a young age, he always wondered what lied within that "spooky old house" in the woods near his grandparents' cottage. In 2016, along with a partner, he formed Ruin Road, a video blog dedicated to exploring abandoned and forgotten buildings. Utilizing his media production degree, he has been dedicated to preserving these beautiful places through film and photographs to tell the history of these places that are now forgotten by most. In his spare time, he enjoys writing screenplays and collecting movies.

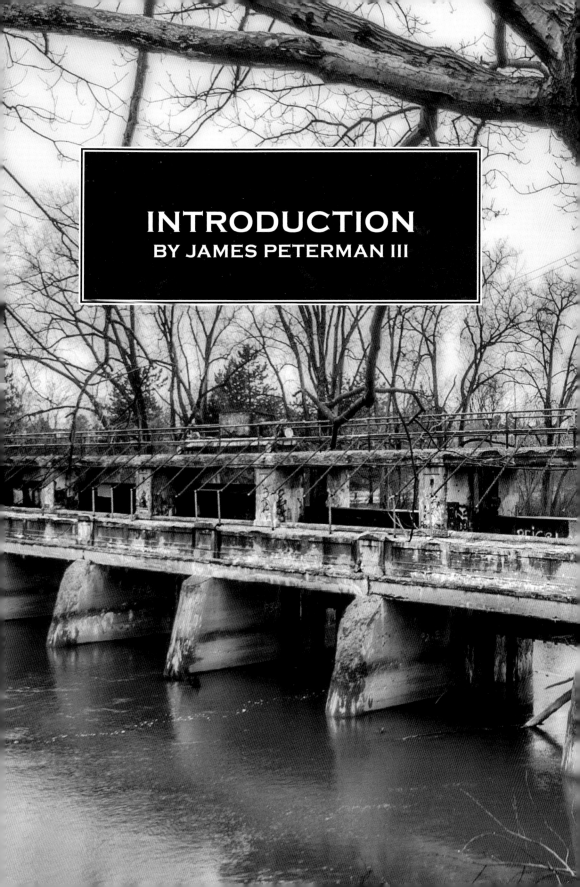

INTRODUCTION
BY JAMES PETERMAN III

T he year was 1819. A fur trader by the name of Jacob Smith founded a small village next to the Flint River. Along with the local Ojibwa tribes and government in that territory, Smith started a trading post in this prosperous lumber town. This became a hotspot for travelers who would frequent the Saginaw Trail as they made the trek between Detroit and Saginaw. By 1855, Flint officially became a city, and it drew in a vast number of people, since lumber was a sought-after commodity around this time. Flint was growing so fast that, by 1860, the U.S. Census recorded that 22,498 of Michigan's 750,000 people resided in this area.

As Flint continued to grow, it became a source of industry for automobiles during the twentieth century. In 1904, a man by the name of William C. Durant came to Flint to manage the Buick Motor Company. Buick became the largest manufacturer of automobiles by 1908, and Durant later founded General Motors. Its headquarters was domiciled in Flint until the 1920s. This city became an epicenter of business for the car industry, and it was booming. By the 1980s, GM hit its peak and it held around 85,000 employees within the company. Around this time, GM began its descent away from Flint, which had been a productive city for providing the manufacturing of vehicles. With a major company harboring a great deal of workers, leaving the city was a move that would take its turn for the worst.

Flint became an epicenter of dangerous and heinous crimes. According to the City-Data website on crime rates, the most recent statistics show that Flint's violent crime rates were almost four times the size of the national average (Flint had 1,083.8 violent crimes compared to the national average of 238.0 in 2017). A large part of this increase in crime has to do with socio-economic issues. The city had a budget deficit of $14.3 million in 2009. With a lack of resources to cover funding for the city, consequently the unemployment rate rose to 14.9 percent and the police force began to dwindle from 265 police on the force in 2007 to only 122 in 2012. This meant that fewer eyes were on the streets to enforce the law, which gave people more free reign to commit crime.

Along with the crime rate and lower population density, Flint also became world-known for another issue dealing with its infrastructure and clean water. In 2014, the city of Flint decided to change its water source from the Detroit River and Lake Huron to the Flint River. This move was made by the city to reduce costs from its original provider to a local source. The plan would save Flint $200 million over twenty-five years. This seemed like a great idea; in the long run, however, the repugnant consequence would end up snowballing into a major health concern for the people residing there.

Citizens of Flint immediately noticed things such as discoloration of their water supply and a metallic smell while running the faucet. By switching to the Flint

River as the source for potable water, high levels of iron accumulated throughout the already aged lead pipes in businesses and homes, causing the alteration of the water. In 2016, the monitoring results for Flint's water confirmed to have had 20 parts per billion (ppb) of lead in the water supply. According to the federal level for safe drinking water standards, that is 5 ppb higher than the limit set by the U.S. Environmental Protection Agency. After five years of aid and refining the infrastructure, Flint's water now has been monitored at reading 4 ppb lead as of 2018, rather than the 20 ppb in the beginning of 2014.

Although a rough estimate of $450 million has been provided to Flint to administer new infrastructure, water quality improvements, education, health care, and other necessary resources, the stigma that Flint has does not make it an enticing city to dwell in by most folks. What was once a flourishing town has inevitably hit rock bottom.

Perhaps there is opportunity for this once automotive producing giant to thrive once again. In the meantime, it remains a troubled place that is vastly seeking solutions to build its wealth and to better its reputation. It is dependent on those who wish to see the city thrive again. It will still take a great deal of work and resources to recover from its current state. Is it truly a lost cause? Only time will tell.

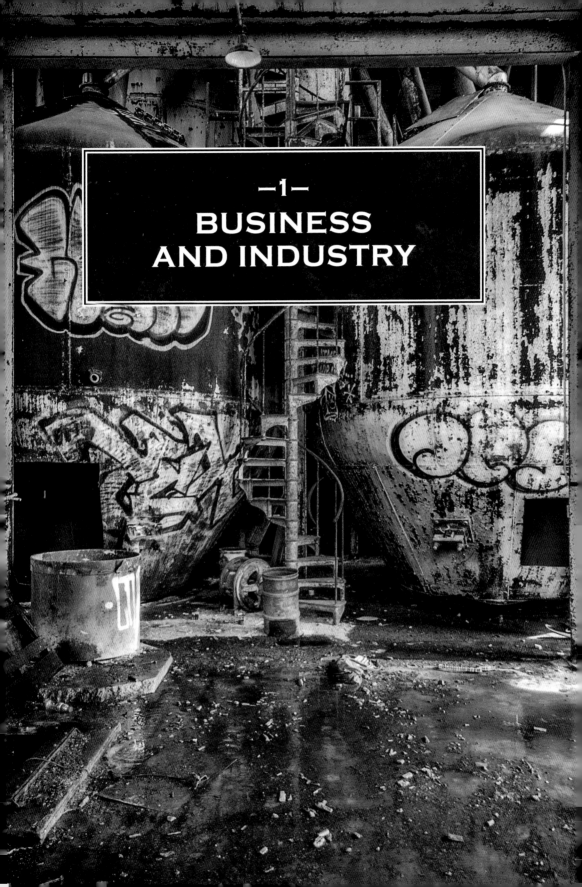

—1—
BUSINESS
AND INDUSTRY

F lint, like so many other large cities, grew around its industry. Beginning as a trade post between Saginaw and Detroit, it grew to become a major player in the lumber industry, in no small part due to the Flint River used to feed the logs to the mills. At the same time, automotive pioneers William Durant and Dallas Dort got their beginnings in the transportation industry with the Durant-Dort Carriage Company.

Near the turn of the century would see the founding of the Buick Motor Company, and in 1910 General Motors was founded. For the first quarter of the twentieth century, Flint would see the creation and absorption of a number of automotive companies, a great deal more than this short book could do justice to chronicling. Instead, I will summarize it by saying the auto industry in Flint *boomed*.

But what brought the city up would also be its demise: Flint's dependence upon this single industry, in particular a single company—GM. At one time, the city had the highest median income in the state, thanks to the high union wages an automotive job provided. But this reason, coupled with the increasing internationalization of the auto industry, led GM and other auto giants to disinvest from the cities they grew up in, none more so than Flint and Detroit.

This deindustrialization led to a number of its citizens to move with the jobs, while others were faced with poverty. From this, a trickle-down effect occurred—small businesses could no longer remain afloat with a lowered clientele, and, in turn, went out of business. This then led to lowered tax revenue for the city, which, in turn, was faced with cutting jobs and scaling back public services. To start looking at how Flint came to the state it is in now, we must first look at the single-most prominent cause—its business and industry.

FISHER PLANT 1 ADMINISTRATION BUILDING

Amidst a complex of pharmacy and health buildings sits a disused four-story building, once the hub of a major business: Fisher Body. Readers of *Abandoned Detroit* may recall Fisher Body Plant 21, another one of the few remaining Fisher locations, which once totaled forty different complexes across the area. The company was a manufacturer of automobile bodies, eventually becoming a division of General Motors.

This property was initially the headquarters for a different car manufacturer, Durant Motors, started in 1921. It was purchased by Fisher Body in 1926 for the site of its first plant after General Motors purchased sixty percent of the company and began producing auto bodies for GM's Buick plant in Flint. It would soon expand to become the world's largest auto body facility at the time.

But in 1936, the plant entered the history books when its workers began a sit-down at Plant 1, which would quickly spread nationwide to every GM plant. The strike led to GM recognizing the United Auto Workers labor union, which previously had been small and unorganized. The following year saw the UAW's membership grow from just 30,000 to 500,000.

The plant remained in operation, eventually being renamed the B-O-C Flint Body Assembly, until December 1987, when it was officially closed. Demolition occurred the following year, the event forever immortalized as the finale to *Roger & Me*. Many former workers and other Flint residents gathered over the following months to watch their beloved plant be torn down.

But unlike other former factory sites, new life began in a matter of months with the construction of the Great Lakes Technology Center, a low-key research and development facility for GM, which kept its name off and leased several of the new buildings. The only remaining building from the Fisher days was the administration building, which became GM's Regional Personnel Centre. GM sold the entire property in 2009, which has become primarily pharmacy-based; however, the administration building remains vacant.

Swanson's Funeral Home

Greene Home for Funerals was founded in the early 1950s, and was one of Flint's oldest and largest black-owned funeral homes until being sold to the Detroit-based Swanson Funeral Homes in 1995. It became a separate entity in 2013, when Swanson's son, O'Neil Swanson II, took over the Flint business, and the problems began.

The following year, the funeral home was broken into, the thief making off with a vacuum cleaner inside one of the hearses, later ditching it in a parking lot. That same year, Swanson's was fined $10,000 for violations. They were also fined the same amount ten years earlier. The business received scores of complaints, ranging from mixed-up ashes, bodies delivered late to funerals with the wigs and makeup applied to them during the ceremony, to even the wrong body brought out.

In 2015, a director from another funeral home visited to pick up a body being transferred from Swanson's. The man reported a horrifying scene inside the garage, saying it reminded him of a slaughterhouse. State inspectors would visit and verify two unrefrigerated bodies had been left in the garage for as long as five months. A year later, another anonymous tip would lead them back, this time finding ten bodies, with maggots crawling all over.

Finally, Swanson's was shut down in 2017. Police and inspectors searched the property, again finding unrefrigerated bodies stacked in boxes. O'Neill Swanson II had his license revoked as well as that of his businesses. He was further charged with ten felony counts in June 2018 for approving pre-paid services, even though he was not legally authorized to do so, as well as using the money for personal expenses rather than properly depositing it. The following year he was convicted on two of those counts, receiving $75,000 in fines and an eleven-month delayed sentence.

The funeral home has remained abandoned since its closure, scrappers slowly removing the flooring and other valuable items. The unclaimed ashes of almost 200 people were later removed from the property, some dating back to the 1980s. They were laid to rest in a local Catholic cemetery.

Stephenson & Sons Roofing Inc.

In 1977, the current office building, as well as a warehouse, were built on this industrial site, which had been utilized as a demolition dumping ground since earlier that decade. Founded in 1964, the Zack Company utilized the property as a landfill, construction company office, and storage area for construction equipment and supplies until selling the parcel in 1999.

A similar business operated there until 2003. Two years later, it was purchased by the Stephenson Company, a roofing contractor, which also leased some of the property to Michigan Mobile Homes, a manufactured home dismantling facility. A suspected arson fire in 2010 left the warehouse section in ruins, and much of the property became a dumping site for hazardous materials until closing in 2015.

After taxes went unpaid, the county acquired the property. The U.S. Environmental Protection Agency stepped in to remove some of the hazardous substances as well as petroleum contamination; however, more than 100 steel drums of roofing adhesive as well as piles of unknown trash remain. Being located next to the Kearsley Dam, the dumpsite has been monitored closely, being cited for two hazardous waste violations in 1985. Further cleanup has been proposed; however, being that there are apparently no immediate dangers, nothing has been done yet.

BIG D PARTY STORE

Starting life as the uniquely spelled Jame's Fruit Market over half a century ago, this property eventually became the Big D Party Store. Named after its first owner, Donald Lemonds, he ran the grocery and convenience store for more than twenty-four years before selling. The store went to bankruptcy court in 2009, but somehow stayed open under the same owners until 2015. The Abuaita Family C-Store applied for an escrow license in 2017 on the property, but it has remained abandoned.

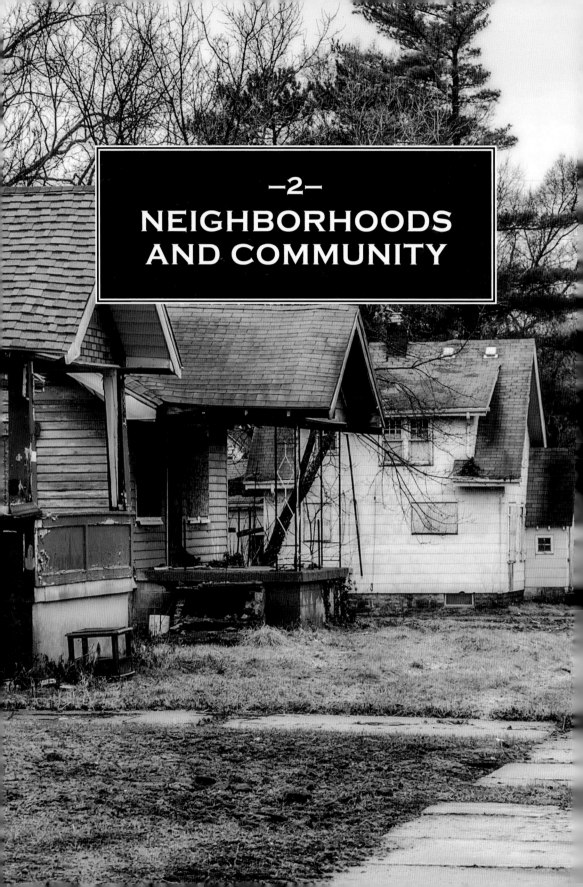

–2–
NEIGHBORHOODS
AND COMMUNITY

The housing crisis of 2008 is cited as being the major factor of abandoned homes in cities such as Cleveland and Detroit, where vacant homes in the city increased 26 percent from 2005 to 2010. The problem in Flint, however, can be traced back much further. With many residents finding themselves laid off in the 1980s from GM, they were unable to pay rent or taxes on their homes. Those that could moved elsewhere where they could find work, but many were left without options when they were evicted. These houses were largely left abandoned, often with much of their previous owner's belongings left inside, as they could only take what they could carry when police showed up to evict them.

Before 1990, vacancy rates were estimated at just six percent, rising steadily until the foreclosure crisis of 2008 drastically increased those rates. This increase in abandonment brought out a new term: hyper-vacancy. Rivaled only by Gary, Indiana, and Cleveland, Ohio, Flint found primarily vacant neighborhoods soar from just 2.5 percent to over 50 percent. This hyper-vacancy created a breeding ground for crime and arson, as well as a domino effect on surrounding property values.

Aided by the federal government, the city has spent tens of millions of dollars on demolitions, but things had not improved much by 2016, when a study found that Flint had the highest number of vacant homes in the entire nation. About one in six homes were empty at that time, totaling almost 10,000. Today, the city continues to demolish what they can, but the problem remains: 42 percent of property in the city remains vacant.

SHADY ACRES

This 200-lot trailer park in north Flint was built in 1950. Residents lived a peaceful life until a management shift in the 2010s would lead to its downfall. Readers of *Abandoned Michigan* may recall the story of the Life O'Reilly trailer park in Lansing, owned by the same man. Like that park, Shady Acres was allowed to deteriorate. In May 2015, residents were shocked to learn the park was foreclosed on, when just the previous month, the owner had collected their rent checks.

After not receiving that money back, many were left unable to move when their utilities were shut off—the owners had left with more than $120,000 in unpaid water and sewage bills. Residents who remained when the weather turned colder were forced to heat their homes with broken pallets and whatever other scrap wood they could find before the landbank stepped in to help move them.

Since then, the park has been used as a dumping ground, every trailer has been badly scrapped, and many have been victims of arson. Due to its size, however, the landbank was reluctant to spend an estimated $150,000 to demolish the property, instead preferring to use that money on easier-to-remove houses. Spurred by petitions from the surrounding community, enough money was finally raised in 2019 to demolish the 20-acre property. The cost? $400,000.

Chester the Molester

Chester Lamar Kelly might not have been born bad, but he didn't take long to become so. Born in 1958, by age twelve he sodomized another boy and was placed on probation. By age fifteen, he had committed the same act at least three more times, as well as several other smaller crimes. His first trip to prison came at age seventeen in Louisiana for forgery.

Returning to Flint, he would run into the law for three weapons charges beginning in 1978, returning to jail in 1986 for three years on assault and intent to commit criminal sexual conduct with a dangerous weapon. Upon being released, Kelly would go on to commit what was called a "one-man crime spree" of an alleged fifteen rapes over the next year until he was caught, his first just twenty days after being paroled.

Using a nylon stocking as a mask, Kelly would focus on young black women with children or relatives living in low-income rental houses along Lapeer Road in south Flint, as well as the neighborhood between ML King and Saginaw streets. He would break into the women's homes, holding them hostage with a pair of long-bladed scissors. In at least one instance, he raped a young mother along with her underage daughter.

Nicknamed "Chester the Molester" by police, he is alleged to have committed more than fifteen rapes during his crime spree, but he was ultimately convicted of just four, along with three breaking and entering charges, with his earliest parole eligibility in 2058.

CARRIAGE TOWN

Located on the north bank of the Flint River, the Carriage Town neighborhood can be called the birthplace of the city. This section is where Jacob Smith built his home in 1819 and had been settled by Native Americans long prior. It is here, too, where GM was first born, with the first offices of the Durant-Dort Carriage Company opening there in 1885.

The neighborhood was inhabited primarily by the company's workers, which would increase exponentially as Durant-Dort became the largest manufacturer of horse-drawn carriages in the world. In 1908, General Motors was formed inside the Durant-Dort offices.

However, unlike GM, Carriage Town did not prosper, and it became the highest-crime neighborhood in the city. By 1982, locals formed the Carriage Town Historic District as a way to organize the community against the abandonment it was beginning to experience. While some homes were restored, still a great number were abandoned by 2015, when a proposal to reduce the size of the historic designation by ten blocks caused a great deal of controversy in the neighborhood.

With the historic designation, the city found an increased difficulty to demolish blighted homes, with the planned shrinking designed to allow more demolitions. In the end, residents succeeded in keeping the area as historic, but the victory was bittersweet, with eight historic houses demolished that same year. Today, Carriage Town is still fighting, many homes have been restored, and the Carriage Town Ministries, a homeless shelter, has weekly neighborhood cleanups by its residents, but there are still many properties left to renovate or remove.

The Durant Dort building has been converted into a museum.

—3—
SCHOOLS

A t one time, the Flint school system was internationally recognized for its community education program, a plan that rose in popularity in the 1930s by a local educator. The system utilized the schools as not only a place to teach its students, but also opened them up for neighborhood and community use, as well as adult education.

By the 1980s, this concept was abandoned due to a lack of funds, but matters would not become drastic until 2007. By that time, Flint schools had suffered from a drop in enrollment and increase in their budget deficit. In Michigan, school aid is given to a district on a per-student basis. Fewer students meant less money. Flint received $159.6 million in 2013. Just four years later, that number had dropped to $41.2 million. In 2012, seven Flint schools were ranked in the bottom five percent of all schools in Michigan.

At its height, the district had 17,867 students in 1968. In 2017, that number had shrunk to just 4,883, just over half of the enrollment in 1915. With the deficit threatening to top $20 million, the district needed to act quickly. At the millennium, the Flint district operated fifty schools. Today, there are just eleven open.

JOHNSON ELEMENTARY

Johnson School opened in 1967, teaching 427 students in grades K-5. It was named after a civic leader and businessman, Donald E. Johnson. The building is unique compared to many Flint schools, which were mainly made of brick, whereas Johnson was constructed using pre-cast concrete paneling with an aluminum top, giving the building the appearance of a bunker. The school would close in 2006, only to be reopened as a private academy, the Johnson Accel Academic Academy. Before closing in 2009, it taught 162 students in grades seven and eight.

Since closing, Johnson School has received more than 100 9-1-1 calls, ranging from drugs, assaults, and break-ins. One such call occurred in 2015, when a sixteen-year-old boy fell through a roof skylight, landing on the gymnasium floor 25 feet below. His younger brother held him while they awaited the arrival of paramedics, but it was too late. The boy was left brain dead and removed from life support later at the hospital.

ZIMMERMAN CENTER

Zimmerman Elementary School opened in 1925. By 1955, it taught 907 students before converting to a middle school by the 1970s. It is also noted that a bold group of 500 whites gathered outside Zimmerman in 1971 to protest the school system's desegregation.

The school remained open through the decades, eventually becoming known as the Zimmerman Center. In 2010, while the city was attempting to save money, it was decided to move Mott Adult High School into the building, and 277 students went to the school, which taught grades 7-12, along with GED and basic adult education classes.

Just three years later, Mott was relocated elsewhere, and Zimmerman was shuttered for good.

Flint Central High School

Flint Central High School opened in 1922, on the grounds of the closed Oak Grove Sanitarium, demolished when the city purchased the 57-acre property in 1919. The new high school replaced the first Flint High School, constructed in 1875. Relocation was considered in the 1960s, but it was decided to remodel the current building instead, adding a new gym and swimming pool with an enclosed walkway to the main building in 1975.

Over the years, CHS produced many professional athletes from an impressive list of sport choices: football, baseball, tennis, wrestling, soccer, swimming, and more. The boys' basketball team won state championships for three consecutive years in the early 1980s. Other extracurricular activities included a theater program and a radio station.

At its height, 2,000 students attended, and some of the notable graduates include U.S. Senator Donald Riegle, *American Top 40* host Casey Kasem, Home Depot CEO Craig Menear, and *American Idol* finalist LaKisha Jones.

But by the 2000s, that number had dropped to less than half in the district's most expensive to operate building. An advisory committee named CHS "the worst facility" in the district with numerous improvements needed, estimated at $27 million. Flint Central and the next-door Whittier Middle School were both closed in 2009.

A 2017 proposal to demolish both schools in order to construct a new, $78.5 million singular high school for the city went nowhere. As yet, the hallways of the three-story school, referred to as "the castle" by its students, remain empty.

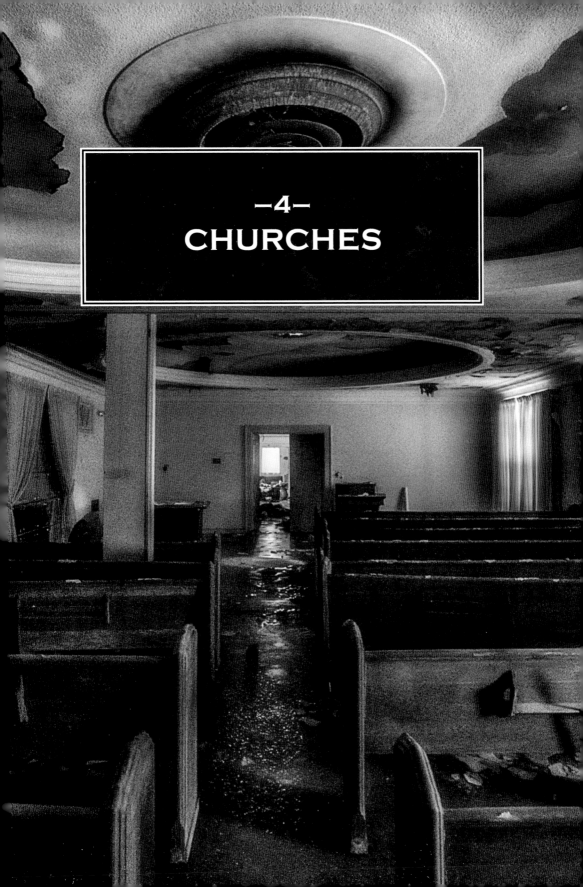

−4−
CHURCHES

As settlers began increasing in number during the 1800s, many began to construct places of worship for themselves and others of likeminded beliefs. By the 1840s, many first congregations had sprung up. These would prove to be too small by the early 1900s as the population grew exponentially, and a great number of churches were expanded while still more opened to accommodate the burgeoning congregations.

Growth would continue, aided in no small part by the high wages enjoyed by factory workers, who could then in turn afford to donate a healthy amount to their church. Many churches would continue to grow into the 1950s, adding additional rooms for community services and schools. But with the city's steady decline after the following decade, the churches too began to see a decrease in donations and worshipers. Many of those that remained were unable to donate as much as their ancestors, as they were struggling to get by themselves.

Left to run the bare essentials inside these once-grand buildings, many began to fall into disrepair. Vandals would break windows that could only be boarded. Some churches could not even operate in their buildings in the winter months, unable to afford heating. Many lifetime attendees were saddened when the Catholic Diocese announced multiple closings due to a growing deficit.

ST. JAMES

St. James Christian Methodist Episcopal Church and Bible Academy was founded in 1980. In 2009, the congregation held an anniversary celebration, featuring a musical performance and service, with the mayor of Saginaw as a guest attendee. The church relocated in 2011, neglecting to pay taxes on the property after that. They announced they would prepare to renovate and remodel the church in 2013, but instead closed permanently that same year. St. James was approved for demolition several years ago, but remains standing.

Oak Park Methodist

Located near the former General Motors plant, this large Neo-Gothic church began the year following the plant's opening in 1908 on land donated by two founders of GM, William C. Durant and J. Dallas Dort. With the neighborhood population increasing to three times its previous size, the first services were held inside a tent before a chapel was constructed in 1910.

The current church building was completed in 1915 and was noted for its impressive lighting and telephone system for the hearing-impaired. A library, chapel, and offices were added in 1969. At its height, the church had a membership of 600 before it closed in 2001.

The building was purchased in 2007 by an up-and-coming nondenominational church in Michigan as one of several new congregations they formed across the state. Focused on outreach, they provided community services, addiction programs, children's ministry, youth groups, nursery, adult education, a food pantry, as well as schooling, before closing in 2015.

ST. AGNES

St. Agnes Catholic Church first began in 1928 with the purchase of twelve and a half acres of land in northwest Flint. Temporary frame buildings were purchased from another nearby Catholic church, but when they were blown down by a windstorm, construction of a permanent two-story church and auditorium began, costing $65,000. The inaugural service was held Thanksgiving Day in 1929 for a congregation of 300 families.

The current church building was completed in 1942, with a unique fan-shape design meant to "develop the devotional, functional, economical, and beautiful attributes" of the property. The former church was then converted into a parish hall and eight-room school, with 350 students taught by the Sisters of St. Joseph, who lived in a convent built on the property that same year.

1948 saw the completion of a four-car garage and rectory with rooms for five priests, three offices, a reception room, kitchen, dining room, and living room. Two years later, a purchase of nearly ten additional acres made space for the construction of a ten-room high school, which opened in 1952.

Post-World War II, the surrounding neighborhood had grown to the point that 1,400 families now attended the church. One thousand children attended St. Agnes' elementary school and 400 at the new high school. To facilitate these new students, wings for an additional twenty nuns were built onto the convent in 1955 and a fourteen-room new high school building was opened in 1958.

But the following decade began to see families leaving the neighborhood, and the St. Agnes High School closed in 1970, when one central Catholic High School consolidated the numerous diocese high schools across the city. In the school's place, they opened both Maurice Olk Elementary School and Donovan North Middle School. As more parishioners continued to leave, St. Agnes joined with six other Catholic parishes to create the Flint Catholic Urban Ministry to better serve the community. The FCUM opened the Father DuKette Catholic School at St. Agnes in 1980 after the Board of Education closed the elementary and middle school.

This alliance kept the church and school going into the 1980s. But by the time of its closure in 2008, the church had less than half the parishioners it had in the mid-1990s. Likewise, the school had a mere sixty-five students in 2006, while 186 were in attendance at the millennium. This, along with financial difficulties, led the diocese to force both to close, along with several other churches in northern Flint.

Since then, the church and convent have been used for services, including a bottled water donation site when the Flint water crisis first arose. But St. Agnes would again come into the public's eye when it was discovered that thousands of cases of the donated water remaining inside the rundown school building.

Sparking outrage, it was uncovered that the building was owned by a closed ministry. The owner's daughter finally spoke out, saying the building was being used as storage by a non-profit group, but a water and sewer main break led to a contamination of the water, which was then left. A giveaway was quickly planned but shut down by the mayor's office, releasing a statement that use of this contaminated water could lead to a public health issue.

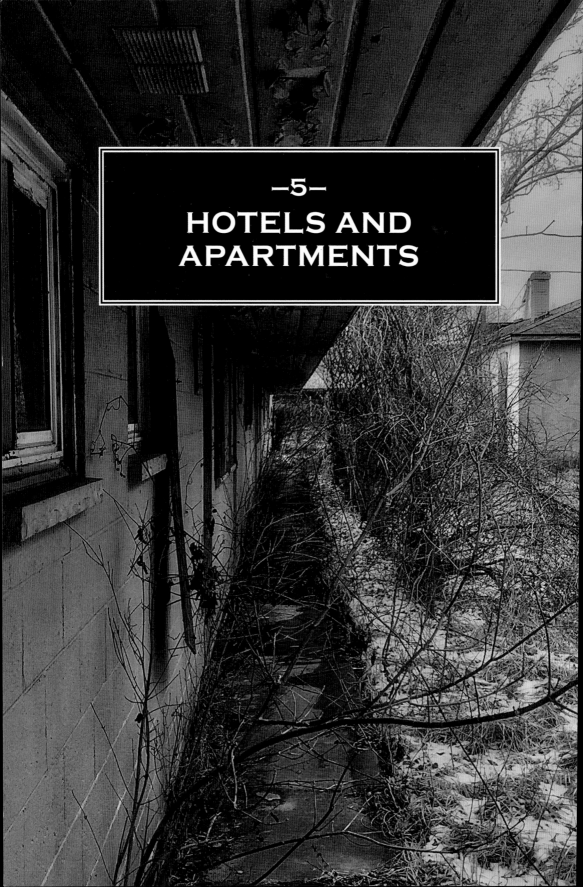

–5–

HOTELS AND
APARTMENTS

F lint has always been a hub of transportation. Not only for products coming in and out for the automotive and other industries, but for people, as well. Corporate travelers as well as vacationing families were drawn to the bustling city at one time and they needed a place to stay. Many hotels such as The Durant sprung up to accommodate. Built in 1920, the magnificent Durant Hotel was a symbol of the city's success as well as decline when it was eventually closed and abandoned.

Likewise, housing for those living in Flint was of importance. Homes were in scarce supply in the rapidly growing city, which saw many apartment complexes built as an alternative to fit more people into the area. When the population's median income range began to drop, many other affordable housing units were constructed, as well.

Most of these have fallen into disrepair from absentee landlords, many content to collect their rent but make little in the way of repairs. Others have simply given up, tired of repairing apartments trashed by temporary occupants. Similar to an abandoned home lowering the value of surrounding houses, those legitimate renters are then forced to suffer as their complex falls into ruin, leading to the city eventually condemning the building and forcing its occupants out.

HOWARD JOHNSON'S

Beginning life in 1970 as the Howawrd Johnson Flint-East Motor Lodge Complex, this hotel was advertised as being attractively close to Buick, Chevrolet, and the AC Spark Plug facilities. It featured 172 rooms, a twenty-four-hour restaurant, indoor pool, tennis courts, color TV, and billiards, located just across the road from the Courtland Center Mall, which opened two years prior.

The hotel would close in 1985 to reopen under numerous chains including Econo Lodge, Travelodge, Budget Host, and America's Best Inn. In later years, the hotel was notoriously rundown, with reports of broken telephones, poor service, and unclean rooms along with armed robberies happening on the property. The health department temporarily shut the pool down for unclean conditions after a guest drowned in the 1990s. Management also withdrew from the Genesee Guest GuaRanTee program, which offers refunds to unsatisfied guests at participating locations.

The restaurant, lodge, and a section of hotel rooms were demolished in 2008 when the land was sold and developed as a strip mall, leaving a single building with seventy rooms. Renovations were announced at this time, but the hotel would close permanently around 2012 after steadily declining revenue over the past decade.

TERRACE TOWNHOUSES/GREENVIEW MANOR

The Cottage Grove Terrace Townhouses were a thirty-four-unit complex consisting of three separate buildings. It eventually became low-income housing, and its name was shortened to simply "Terrace Townhouses" before closing permanently in 2013.

There are reports of minor crimes before closing, but the worst crime occurred in 1996, when two men were shot and killed in the parking lot. One of the men was arguing with the mother of his child, when the woman's brother came out of the building and opened fire with a handgun. The second man, who was sitting in a nearby car, began to return fire before being killed, as well.

The surviving shooter, Khalifah Boyd, was convicted and served nine years. He later confessed to being the shooter in a 1991 cold case crime, taking a plea bargain in return for testifying against two others involved.

Next to Terrace lay the remains of Greenview Manor. Built in 1968, this eighty-four-unit complex had fallen into disrepair by 2001, and the city sold the property to the Mission of Peace Community Development Corporation, which agreed to the necessary $700,000 in renovations, using it as a housing assistance program, while the city converted one building into a mini-station for the Police Department.

By 2009, however, the necessary repairs had not been completed, and the property was declared unsafe. The city allocated $20,000 to assist four families in moving elsewhere while the owner was to renovate. Instead, they abandoned the property the following year and the landbank eventually gained ownership. Greenview has been slated for demolition in 2019, and the land, along with Terrace Townhouses, is being eyed by nearby Kettering University for purchase.

CREEKSIDE APARTMENTS

This sixty-one-unit apartment complex was built in 1965 in a neighborhood just off Dort Highway made up of numerous apartment complexes, mostly built within a few years of each other. Creekside would go downhill, with rodents, crime, squatters, and in 2017: no heat.

For the residents who remained, they watched their buildings crumble around them, as a broken water pipe in one apartment went unfixed, leading to growing mold and a section of the ceiling to collapse. Most residents had moved out during the winter months, but some had no choice but to stay. The management company claimed it had replaced the boiler multiple times, only to have scrappers steal it.

Eventually, the few remaining tenants were moved out and the complex closed in 2018. The following year, the apartments would come on the city's radar again when the illegal dumping had gotten so bad that the entire parking lot was literally piled high with trash, sparking anger from those living in the other apartments on the same street. The owners were fined, which amounted to nothing as they lived out of state and had a disconnected phone number. Cleanup eventually fell onto the city, which cleared multiple dumpster loads from the property.

—6—
HEALTH AND GOVERNMENT

The government of Flint has been under heavy scrutiny from the time leading up to the water crisis and onward, but there is far more history than just that. From the time of its incorporation as a city, there were differences in opinions on the city. A 1885 newspaper article points out that Flint had a higher population than that of Adrian and a similar population to that of Grand Rapids at the time of their incorporations, but many in the community preferred Flint to only become a charter village.

After several hours of heated debate, it was decided that Flint was to become a city, an argument that would prove null with the population boom the following century. City services grew to accommodate its citizens, with advancements such as the school system gaining nationwide notoriety. The fire department, likewise, began to push toward fire prevention rather than fire control in the 1950s, making them the first in the nation to do so.

The Flint city planners estimated that the following decade would see the population expand to 250,000, and began to prepare government departments accordingly. Ultimately, Flint's population had already peaked by that point and the estimates proved drastically wrong as the population began to decrease. Left now with a larger system than needed, Flint found itself with a debt of $30 million by 2002 and its control was taken over by the state for the first time that year.

In a cost-saving measure, city ambulance services were ended along with massive layoffs and consolidations. Departments such the fire department, which was previously operating ten stations, now had to cover the entire city with just three. The state governor would declare the city in financial emergency again in 2011, cutting budgets yet again.

This time, cuts left only 122 police officers to watch over the city, roughly one for every 830 citizens. For comparison, New York City employs one officer for every 235. Flint exited state control in 2015, but many problems remained. Further cuts in 2017 left just 100 officers for the city.

FLINT REGIONAL POLICE TRAINING ACADEMY

Across the train tracks and an overgrown field from the leveled Buick City plant sits the remains of the former Flint Police Academy. Featuring a shooting range, driving simulator, classrooms, and a gymnasium, the academy turned out a number of soon-to-be police officers for the city.

The property began life as a boarding house. The 1926 city directory lists three boarders including a farmer, student, and someone simply called "Louise." By 1956, it had become the Epsilon Upsilon Lambda fraternity house. With the neighborhood's shift into more industrial buildings, the house was eventually leveled, and an air quality monitoring business operated there through the 1980s.

Next it became the Flint Police Academy, one of only four academies in Michigan that exclusively trained officers for their specific cities. One of the former directors of the school was elected as Flint's chief of police in 2007, around the same time that the training program was relocated to Mott Community College.

The building was still used, though primarily for community training programs, such as block clubs and the Blue Badge Volunteers, which trained citizens in traffic control to assist police during major events, as well as administrative duties and community relations functions. The building was closed for good in 2014 to cut department costs. Today, paramedics park their ambulances outside, and the occasional police officer will have a lunch break outside the shuttered building where they learned their profession.

FIRE STATION NO. 4

The Flint Fire Department began in 1855, when the city was first incorporated. Additional stations were added as the city grew, and in 1916 Fire Station No. 4 is noted as having both a horse-drawn truck and automobile hose car. A spare hose wagon was available to be drawn behind the car if needed.

The station eventually was relocated several blocks from its original location, though it remained a two-truck station when built, eventually downsizing to one truck. A 2003 report conducted for the city notes that Station 4 was in severe disrepair and likely the oldest station still in use. Seven years later, the station was the first of four Flint fire stations closed when federal grant money ran out. With an average of 486 arson fires a year, the city was left with only half of their stations operational. In the years since, only one station was reopened.

In less than a year of its closure, scrappers had broken in and stolen the boiler system and copper piping. The city attempted to lease the property in 2016 with no luck.

Feminine Health Care Clinic

 In 2009, a news story spread nationwide of a forced abortion that occurred in the Feminine Health Care Clinic of Flint. In 2008, an eighteen-year-old high school dropout went to the clinic planning to get an abortion from Dr. Abraham Alberto Hodari. Things went as planned until on the operating table she expressed that she had changed her mind, but Hodari continued anyway. There were conflicting reports on whether it was too late to stop or not, but that was not the first time Hodari had come under fire.

 Opening his first clinic in 1980, Hodari owned as many as fourteen across Michigan by 1988. They were listed on the recommended list of safe clinics by the National Abortion Federation, but by 2009 had been removed from the list for undisclosed reasons.

 Hodari was quoted in a lecture at Wayne State University in 2007 saying that doctors are allowed to lie to their patients. That same year, the Michigan Department of Community Health accused him of negligence in the death of a patient and at least three others are known to have died from his procedures. He has been sued more than fifty times, including for such things as missing an ectopic pregnancy and leaving a baby's head inside the mother. Pro-life supporters found patient records and the remains of aborted fetuses outside another one of his clinics. Multiple other women have reported that Hodari either tricked or forced them to have abortions at as young an age as sixteen.

 With weekly protests outside this and his other clinics, Hodari allowed his license to expire and closed the buildings in 2013. Two years later, the building was discovered to still house tens of thousands of confidential patient records; however, by the time a detective was sent to investigate—weeks later—the boxes had been removed. However, bags of medical waste and hundreds of other documents remained in the unsecured building.

 Six months after closing his practice, Hodari reapplied for his license but it was denied. The forced-abortion lawsuit was settled out of court.

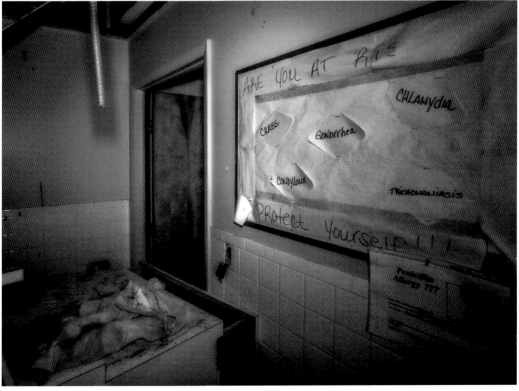

FLINT WATER TREATMENT PLANT

Like many government services today, the water distribution system began as a private company. The Flint Water Works Company began in 1883 and installed all lead pipes after a city ordinance declared all water main connections be made with them. The company operated until it was purchased by the city in 1912. Five years later, a new plant was constructed and was treating nearly 20,000 gallons of Flint River water per minute by 1930.

The growing population necessitated the addition of a second plant in 1952. Located beside the older plant, the two pumped out 100 million gallons of treated water per day. Both plants operated simultaneously until 1967, when Flint began to purchase pre-treated Lake Huron water from the Detroit Water and Sewage Department as a result of the degradation of water quality in the Flint River from the numerous industries located along it, which were unregulated at that time.

The original plant was closed while the newer building was only used several times a year as a backup facility. It would remain this way until undergoing renovations in 2014 to reopen as a full-time water treatment plant for the city, and the troubles began.

–7–
ATTRACTIONS AND ENTERTAINMENT

A fter World War II, Flint began to enter as one of the nation's centers for modern culture. Led by the Mott Foundation, Flint's Cultural Center was founded, which featured an automotive and art museum, as well as a library, planetarium, and performing arts and music center. In 1956, the University of Michigan Flint Campus began with just 167 students, but it has grown to 8,600 today. Opening in 1965, the Sloan Museum continues to operate to this day, too.

But not all of Flint's attractions and entertainment have fared as well. With the city losing its revenue from GM's departure, city leaders knew they had to diversify Flint's dependence on a singular economy. Leaders decided that, in order to save Flint, they needed to reinvent the city as a tourist destination. A massive push to create these attractions saw such developments as the Hyatt Regency Hotel and the AutoWorld theme park. Built at a cost of $80 million, AutoWorld was designed as a tribute to the automobile, but like GM, the automobile was done with Flint. The park proved to be an immediate flop. It was never open more than six months at a time and closed permanently just two years after opening in 1984.

The Hyatt, too, had a hard time attracting any big events to its convention center. They were forced to settle for things such as Scrabble conventions before going bankrupt, as well. The entire debacle ended up costing both the Mott Foundation and taxpayers several hundred million dollars.

It seems the city has not learned from its mistakes, as more recently the state and Flint's Convention and Visitors Bureau spent $200,000 in 2008 on a radio ad featuring Michigan-native and comedian Tim Allen. The ad elicited more laughs than booked plane tickets.

PIRATES PARK

Behind a busy commercial strip is the overgrown remains of Pirates Park, an amusement center once bringing entertainment to families, now quiet save for the passing cars of the nearby highway.

The park began construction in 1991, featuring the Typhoon water slide, bungee jump, bumper boats, mini golf, arcade, batting cages, go-carts, and refreshment area. Many locals fondly remember spending summer days and evenings at the park, which even hosted a millennium fireworks show in 2000.

However, the new millennium could not draw in the crowds the previous decade had, and the summer of 2015 saw the park open on weekends only before closing permanently after the season. The owners, a married couple, tried reopening the indoor section several times as an inflatable bounce house and hosted private children's parties to no luck; the final nail came when the husband passed away.

The property has been eyed several times in the following years, being announced as a hotel, storage facility, and assisted-living center, as well as reopening as a city-run park. But, as of yet, the only admission price to visitors of this park is a trespassing ticket.

WINDMILL PLACE

One of the city's pushes for tourism, Windmill Place opened in 1982 as an enclosed, upscale international dining and shopping marketplace. Costing $3.7 million, the mall was just a portion of the River Village redevelopment project, which also saw the construction of a high-rise exclusively for the elderly and an apartment complex adjacent to Windmill Place.

Consisting of four buildings, Building A featured fifteen eateries as well as numerous specialty shops. Building B was a larger restaurant and bar. Building C was retail space, and Building D was planned as a pharmacy and supermarket to accommodate those living in the nearby buildings. After no grocers or pharmacists were interested, it was converted into office space and then leased to GM. Also on the property was the Electric Avenue Arcade.

The same time AutoWorld closed, Windmill Place would go bankrupt. It was purchased by a local entrepreneur who would go on to unsuccessfully run for mayor in 1991. He did manage to keep Windmill Place operational, even securing a performance by rapper Tupac Shakur in 1993 alongside local rapper Jake the Flake. The office space went on to become the Coordinated Campaign HQ, which was used as a rally spot for Governor Jennifer Granholm, U.S. Senator Debbie Stabenow, and several others in 2006.

The following year, Building A was torn down to make way for a Family Dollar store. Talks of expansion and redevelopment of further buildings were mentioned, but nothing occurred. Family Dollar eventually closed in 2019. The rest of Windmill Place has been closed for years, no longer owned by that local entrepreneur, who did eventually become mayor in 2003.

BOGNER SOUND & MUSIC

Bogner's was a musical instrument and sound system retailer opened in 1992, offering service and repairs, as well. They sold and installed home theater systems, church audio systems, band equipment, and more. The original building Bogner's would be housed in was built in sections, with the first retail shop opening in 1930. Two more retail sections were added in 1948 and back storage sections were constructed in 1954 before all sections merged into Bogner's.

The store is fondly remembered by many as being a friendly, no pressure, mom-and-pop store. It closed in 2016 and its owner passed away the next year. The building was owned by his father, who died in 2016. After taxes went unpaid following their deaths, the landbank assumed ownership.

LUGE BAR

Constructed as a bank in 1958, this three-story building would eventually be converted into the Korner Bar on the first floor, with apartments on the upper floors. Located across from Fisher Body 1, it was a frequent hangout for the United Auto Workers union members. In 1980, the building caught the attention of a shop worker at Fisher. Nearing retirement, the man decided to take a chance and purchase the bar, having no previous business experience.

Despite his trepidations, the bar succeeded. The winter months were noted as being particularly popular, giving locals a chance to get out and socialize. Euchre tournaments and other events would be held on the weekends. In 1984, the bar is noted as being the scene of some tensions when the mainly Democratic union workers were horrified and angered to find some of their younger drinking companions in favor of re-electing President Ronald Reagan.

It would again see reporters flocking to interview patrons with the announcement of Fisher's closure in 1987. Unlike the adjacent Ethel's Bar, which closed upon hearing the news, the owner of the Korner Bar did not have that luxury; all of his investments were tied into the property. Sadly, he could not keep the bar open and sold the property.

It next became The Bank Bar before ending as the Luge Bar & High-Country Saloon. All three floors were converted into club space, and an outdoor patio was added. Many residents fondly remember the bar, which featured open mic night on Wednesdays, and karaoke on Thursdays. A fire in 2009 saw the club permanently closed.

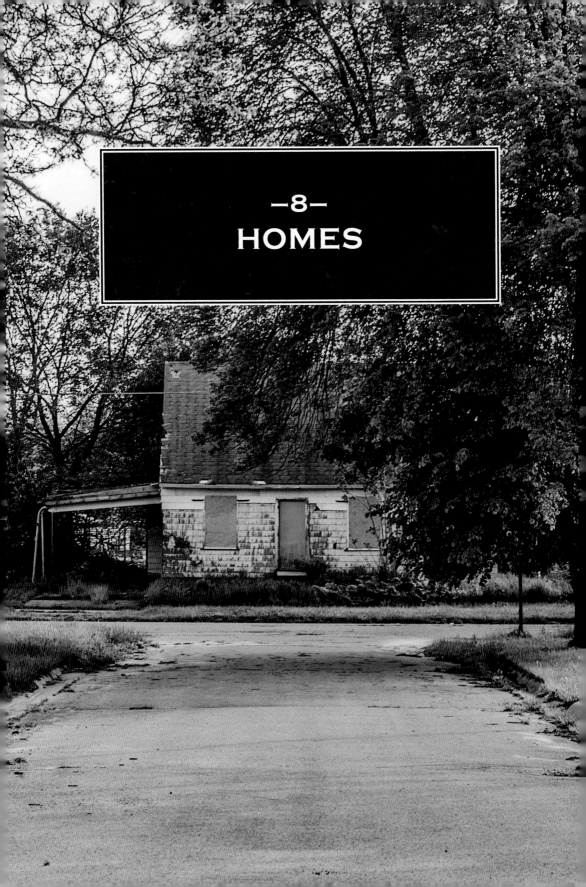

–8–
HOMES

Livingston Home

This five-bedroom, four-bath home was built in 1926. The original owners are obscured through time; however, in the late 1930s, the Livingstons occupied it, a Jewish family from Germany. They were prompted to move to America after their high school daughter was detained by the Nazi SS while at a store, only being let go because she looked much younger than her actual age.

Upon hearing this, the family decided to move, finding a family to sponsor them in Flint. At that time, Nazi Germany would only allow Jews to leave the country with a small amount of money and personal property, thus requiring a stateside sponsor to take responsibility for them. It seems the older son wasted no time upon arriving, as he was engaged to a Flint Central High School and University of Michigan graduate in 1938.

After marrying, the pair moved to their own home elsewhere in the city. Once the rest of the family was established enough to own their own residence, they moved to Chicago where the daughter would get married in 1944. The house would change hands over the years, eventually converting into a small nursing home by the early 1990s.

In 2019, the city pledged $200,000 to help improve the neighborhood. A plan which seems to include the former house, which has sat vacant for over a decade at this point, would convert it into a neighborhood center.

THE SLAIN WOMAN

Located just outside the also-abandoned Ambassador East Mobile Home Park, this house was built in 1949. On March 20, 1994, the body of its owner was found behind the Richfield Bowl just east of Flint. She was one of three prostitutes found murdered between 1993 and 1994 in the area. A man living in Grand Blanc Township previously convicted of kidnapping and rape was suspected but never charged. Police also mentioned the women might have been victims of a serial killer who may have been arrested on another charge, thus taking a forced break from killing.

In later years, an elderly couple purchased the home, which is likely when the addition of the wheelchair ramp was made. The husband worked at GM for twenty years, and the pair had three children and four grandchildren. The home was last occupied in 2012 and has since been approved for demolition.

AROUND TOWN

This twenty-six-room mansion was built in 1926 by local businessman Jonathan Burroughs.

BIBLIOGRAPHY

"Andrew Bogner Obituary." *Flint Journal*, 20 Dec. 2017, obits.mlive.com/obituaries/flint/obituary.
   aspx?n=andrew-bogner-andy&pid=187567236&fhid=25621.

"About CTHNA." *Carriage Town Historic Neighborhood Association*, 2019, cthna.org/.

Acosta, Roberto. "Multimillion-Dollar Project Planned for Flint Township's Pirate's Park." *Mlive.Com*,
   20 Nov. 2015, www.mlive.com/news/flint/2015/11/multi-million_dollar_developme.html.

Acosta, Roberto. "New Middle School, High School Discussed at Former Flint Central High Site."
   Mlive.Com, 29 July 2016, www.mlive.com/news/flint/2016/07/new_middle_school_high_school.html.

Acosta, Roberto. "Pirate's Park in Flint Township Was a Cool Place to Enjoy Summer Chill Out." *Mlive.
   Com*, 24 Nov. 2015, www.mlive.com/news/flint/2015/11/pirates_park_in_flint_township.html.

Adams, Dominic. "Here's How Flint Went from Boom Town to Nation's Highest Poverty Rate." *Mlive.
   Com*, 21 Sept. 2017, www.mlive.com/news/flint/2017/09/heres_how_flint_went_from_boom.html.

Adams, Dominic. "The Rise and Fall of Flint School District Enrollment over a Century." *Mlive.Com*, 7
   Oct. 2015, www.mlive.com/news/flint/2015/10/see_ebb_and_flow_of_flint_scho.html.

Adams, Dominic. "Triggerman Admits to Cold Case Killing, Turns Witness against Two Others." *Mlive.
   Com*, 27 June 2018, www.mlive.com/news/flint/2018/06/trigger_man_in_1991_cold_case.html.

AlHajal, Khalil. "Flint Fire Stations Could Shut down after Demotions This Weekend." *Mlive.Com*, 20
   Jan. 2011, www.mlive.com/news/flint/2011/01/flint_fire_stations_could_shut.html.

AlHajal, Khalil. "Mott Adult High School to Add Location, Reduce Presence at Broome Center." *Mlive.
   Com*, 12 June 2010, www.mlive.com/news/flint/2010/06/mott_adult_high_school_to_add.html.

Allen, E.B. "Flint Launches $200,000 Martin Luther King Neighborhood Improvement
   Plan - The Hub Flint." *The HUB Flint*, 2 May 2019, www.thehubflint.com/
   city-launches-200000-martin-luther-king-neighborhood-improvement-plan/.

Burden, Melissa. "Part of America's Best Inn Makes Way for New Strip Mall." *Mlive.Com*, 8 July 2008,
   www.mlive.com/flintjournal/business/2008/07/part_of_americas_best_inn_make.html.

Carmody, Steve. "Flint's Carriage Town Neighborhood Weighs Proposal to Shrink
   Its Historic District." *MichiganRadio*, 2015, www.michiganradio.org/post/
   flints-carriage-town-neighborhood-weighs-proposal-shrink-its-historic-district.

Collins, Si U, et al. *The Flint Fire Department : Past and Present*. Flint, Mich., Flint Printing Co, 1916.

Conat, Randy. "House Demolition Begins in Flint's Carriage Town Historic Neighborhood." *Abc12.
   Com*, 2015, www.abc12.com/home/headlines/House-demolition-begins-in-Flints-Carriage-Town-
   Historic-Neighborhood-321317321.html.

Cook, Rebecca. *Flint Has Highest Rate of Vacant Homes in United States:
   Report*. Reuters, 11 Feb. 2016, www.reuters.com/article/us-flint-vacancies/
   flint-has-highest-rate-of-vacant-homes-in-united-states-report-idUSKCN0VK08L.

Crawford, Kim. "Serial Criminals Have Plagued Area Over Past 20 Years." *The Flint Journal*, 24 Oct. 1999.

"Crime in Flint, Michigan." *City-Data.Com*, 2017, www.city-data.com/crime/crime-Flint-Michigan.html.

Custer, Nic, and Jan Worth-Nelson. "Residents Air Concerns about Central High School Demolition, Replacement." *East Village Magazine*, 6 Feb. 2017.

Dandaneau, Steven P. *A Town Abandoned : Flint, Michigan, Confront Deindustrialization*. Albany N.Y., State University Of New York Press, 1996.

"Engagements." *The Detroit Jewish Chronicle*, 7 Jan. 1938, p. 8.

"Flint Central High School." *Wikipedia*, Wikimedia Foundation, 28 Apr. 2019, en.wikipedia.org/wiki/Flint_Central_High_School#cite_ref-3.

Flint City Directory. Detroit, MI, R. L. Polk & Co., 1922.

Flint, Many. "Many Flint Autoworkers Support Reagan, Threatening Old Democratic Stronghold." *UPI*, 28 Oct. 1984, www.upi.com/Archives/1984/10/28/Many-Flint-autoworkers-support-Reagan-threatening-old-Democratic-stronghold/9115467784000/.

"Flint Water - Taking Action on Flint Water." *Michigan.Gov*, 2017, www.michigan.gov/flintwater.

Florida, Richard. "How Vacancy Traumatizes Cities." *CityLab*, 30 July 2018, www.citylab.com/equity/2018/07/vacancy-americas-other-housing-crisis/565901/.

Fonger, Ron. *Abandoned Mobile Home Parks Create New Headaches for Flint*. mlive.com, 27 Apr. 2015, www.mlive.com/news/flint/2015/04/abandoned_flint_mobile_home_pa.html.

Fonger, Ron. "Operator of Shuttered Flint Funeral Home Gets More Time to Discuss Possible Plea." *Mlive.Com*, 26 Apr. 2019, www.mlive.com/news/flint/2019/04/operator-of-shuttered-flint-funeral-home-gets-more-time-to-discuss-possible-plea.html.

Foren, John. "Long-Time Parishioners Mourn Closings of Three Flint Churches." *Mlive.Com*, 9 June 2008, www.mlive.com/news/flint/2008/06/longtime_parishioners_mourn_cl.html.

Hardmon, Cheri. "Multimillion-Dollar Project Planned for Flint Township's Pirate's Park." *Abc12.Com*, 20 Nov. 2015, www.abc12.com/content/news/Old-amusement-park-could-reopen-in-Flint-Township-477312543.html.

Harris, David. "Flint Police to Start Another Round of Blue Badge Volunteer Corps Training Sessions." *Mlive.Com*, 15 Feb. 2012, www.mlive.com/news/flint/2012/02/flint_police_to_start_another.html.

Highsmith, Andrew R. *Demolition Means Progress : Flint, Michigan, and the Fate of the American Metropolis*. Chicago, The University Of Chicago Press, 2016.

"History of UM-Flint | University of Michigan-Flint." *Umflint.Edu*, UM-Flint, 2010, www.umflint.edu/history-um-flint.

Holice, Deb, and Clayton Holice. "The History of Genesee, MI, Chap. 27, Religious Organizations, Part I." *Usgennet.Org*, 2019, www.usgennet.org/usa/mi/county/lapeer/gen/ch27/pt1.html.

Holice, Deb, and Clayton Holice. "The History of Genesee, MI, Chapter 13, Early Years of Flint City." *Usgennet.Org*, 2019, www.usgennet.org/usa/mi/county/lapeer/gen/ch13/earlyflint1.html.

IJN Staff. "Annelie Sherwood." *IJN*, Intermountain Jewish News, 27 May 2016, www.ijn.com/annelie-sherwood/.

Jackson, David D. "Fisher Body Flint Plant One in World War Two." *American Automobile Industry in World War Two*, 8 Sept. 2018, www.usautoindustryworldwartwo.com/Fisher%20Body/fisherbodyflintone.htm.

Jaeger, Sarah. "Neighbors Fed up after Piles of Trash Dumped at Abandoned Apartments." *NBC25News*, WEYI, 2 May 2019, nbc25news.com/news/local/neighbors-fed-up-after-piles-of-trash-dumped-at-abandoned-apartments.

Kearns, Josie. *Life after the Line*. Detroit, Wayne State University Press, 1990.

Kennedy, Merrit. "Lead-Laced Water In Flint: A Step-By-Step Look At The Makings Of A Crisis." *Npr.Org*, 20 Apr. 2016, www.npr.org/sections/thetwo-way/2016/04/20/465545378/lead-laced-water-in-flint-a-step-by-step-look-at-the-makings-of-a-crisis.

Kummerlowe, Richard. "Flint-East." *Highwayhost.Org*, 2010, www.highwayhost.org/Michigan/Flint/East/East1.htm.

Lawlor, Joe. "New $200,000 Radio Ad on Tourism in Flint and Michigan Features Comedian Tim Allen as Narrator." *Mlive.Com*, 17 Apr. 2008, www.mlive.com/news/flint/2008/04/xxxxxxx_joes_tourism_story_xxx.html.

Lazovic, Brandon. "The Rise And Fall Of Flint, Michigan Beginning In The 1800s." *The Odyssey Online*, 17 Feb. 2016, www.theodysseyonline.com/rise-fall-flint-michigan-beginning-1800s.

Longley, Kristin. "City of Flint to Relocate Four Residents from 'unsafe' Apartment Complex." *Mlive.Com*, 27 Oct. 2009, www.mlive.com/flint-city-beat/2009/10/city_of_flint_to_relocate_four.html.

Longley, Kristin. "Flint Central High School Faces Uncertain Future." *Mlive.Com*, 8 Mar. 2009, www.mlive.com/news/flint/2009/03/flint_central_high_school_face.html.

Longley, Kristin. "Soon-to-Close Schools Were Cornerstones of Flint History." *Mlive.Com*, 2 May 2009, www.mlive.com/news/flint/2009/05/soontoclose_schools_were_corne.html.

Lord, George F., and Albert C. Price. "Growth Ideology in a Period of Decline: Deindustrialization and Restructuring, Flint Style." *Social Problems*, vol. 39, no. 2, May 1992, pp. 155–169.

Mcelmurry, Shawn P., et al. "Flint Water Crisis: What Happened and Why?" *American Waterworks Association*, vol. 108, no. 12, Dec. 2016, pp. 22–34, awwa.onlinelibrary.wiley.com/doi/abs/10.5942/jawwa.2016.108.0195, 10.5942/jawwa.2016.108.0195.

Moore, Andrew. "Residents at Apartment Complex in Flint Living without Heat for Months, Now No Water." *NBC25News*, WEYI, 5 Jan. 2018, nbc25news.com/news/local/residents-at-apartment-complex-in-flint-living-without-heat-for-months-now-no-water.

Morrison, Julie. "Two-Story Building at Windmill Place to Be Torn Down." *Mlive.Com*, 2 Nov. 2007, blog.mlive.com/flintjournal/newsnow/2007/11/twostory_building_at_windmill.html.

"Oak Park Methodist Episcopal Church - MichMarkers." *Michmarkers.Com*, 2019, www.michmarkers.com/default?page=L1861.

ogoodins@mlive.com, Oona Goodin-Smith. "Flint's History of Emergency Management and How It Got to Financial Freedom." *Mlive.Com*, 16 Jan. 2018, www.mlive.com/news/flint/2018/01/city_of_the_state_flints_histo.html.

Parkinson, Stephanie. "Criminal Investigation into Former Owner of Flint Mobile Home Parks." WEYI, 22 Apr. 2015, nbc25news.com/news/local/criminal-investigation-into-former-owner-of-flint-mobile-home-parks.

Phi, Alpha. "Graduate Chapters." The Sphinx, vol. 42, no. 1, Feb. 1956, p. 46, issuu.com/apa1906network/docs/195604201/, 195604201.

Putnam, Judy. "Putnam: Cemetery Trying to Return Ashes to Families of Nearly 200 Deceased Found in Closed Flint Funeral Home." Lansing State Journal, 10 Mar. 2018, www.lansingstatejournal.com/story/opinion/columnists/judy-putnam/2018/03/10/putnam-laying-dead-restforgotten-ashes-found-troubled-flint-funeral-home-but-one-lansing-woman-not/408445002/.

Rauschert, Jeff. "Flint-Area Club Listing." Mlive.Com, 14 Mar. 2008, www.mlive.com/flintjournal/entertainment/2008/03/flintarea_club_listing.html.

Raymer, Marjory. "Flint Businessman Leo Greene Remembered for Generosity." Mlive.Com, 2 Apr. 2008, www.mlive.com/flintjournal/newsnow/2008/04/flint_businessman_leo_greene_r.html.

Raymer, Marjory. "Flint Central High School History Not Necessarily Over." Mlive.Com, 25 Apr. 2009, www.mlive.com/opinion/flint/2009/04/flint_central_high_school_hist.html.

Ridley, Gary. "Empty School Buildings in Flint Now Magnets for Crime and Arson." Mlive.Com, 1 Oct. 2015, www.mlive.com/news/flint/2015/10/closed_flint_schools_become_ho.html?

Schuch, Sarah. "School's out: Flint School Closures to Displace More than 2,000 Students." Mlive.Com, 15 Mar. 2013, www.mlive.com/news/flint/2013/03/schools_out_flint_school_closu.html.

Smedley, Ronald, and Paul Bucholtz. "Draft Analysis of Brownfield Cleanup Alternatives Former Zack Company Demo Dump." MDEQ Remediation and Redevelopment Division, 4 Jan. 2019.

Smith, James L., and Kim Crawford. "Tracking Path of Serial Killers Takes Teamwork." *The Flint Journal*, 24 Oct. 1999.

Tewksbury, Mary. "Religion Notes." *Mlive.Com*, 30 Oct. 2009, www.mlive.com/living/flint/2009/10/religion_notes_15.html.

Thorne, Blake. "Closing Flint's Middle Schools, Three Elementary Schools under Discussion by Flint School Board." *Mlive.Com*, 3 May 2012, www.mlive.com/news/flint/2012/05/closing_flints_middle_schools.html.

Troppens, Anna. "The Freedom Center Plans $3 Million in Renovations." *Tri County Times*, 24 Mar. 2011, www.tctimes.com/living/the-freedom-center-plans-million-in-renovations/article_48439ff6-6e99-50ef-87cf-934f543cb46c.html.

"What Did Refugees Need to Obtain a US Visa in the 1930s?" *Ushmm.Org*, United States Holocaust Memorial Museum, 2018, exhibitions.ushmm.org/americans-and-the-holocaust/what-did-refugees-need-to-obtain-a-us-visa-in-the-1930s.

Worth-Nelson, Jan. "42 Percent Vacant: Forum Explores Flint's 'Everyday Remaking of Place' after Abandonments." *East Village Magazine*, 8 Feb. 2018.

Young, Gordon. "Faded Glory: Polishing a City's Jewels." *The New York Times*, 19 Aug. 2009, www.nytimes.com/2009/08/20/garden/20flint.html.

Young, Gordon. "From Fruit to Freeway." *Flintexpats.Com*, 2014, www.flintexpats.com/2008/08/from-fruit-to-freeway.html.

Young, Molly. "Hearse Stolen from Flint Funeral Home Found in Old Value City Parking Lot." *Mlive.Com*, 13 Nov. 2014, www.mlive.com/news/flint/2014/11/hearse_stolen_from_swanson_fun.html.

Flint Fire Department. 2003, *Flint Fire Department*, icma.org/sites/default/files/2036_.pdf.

Roedel, Colin. "A Look into the Trials, Tribulations of Flint City Police." The Michigan Times, 1 Feb. 2018.

Ertelt, Steven. "Abortionist Left Thousands of Patient Records at Abandoned Abortion Clinic." Lifenews.com, 31 Mar. 2015.

Dupnack, Jessica. "Medical Records Abandoned at Former Flint Abortion Clinic." *ABC12*, 27 Mar. 2015.

Ridley, Gary. "Flint Abortion Clinic That Made National News Closes Its Doors." *Mlive*, 4 Sept. 2013.

Russell, Kim. "Doctor Accused of Forced Abortion Has Troubled Past." NBC25News, 26 May 2010.

Gantert, Tom. "MLive Erroneously Reports New Flint Police Officers Get Just $11.25/Hour." Michigan Capitol Confidential, 19 Sept. 2017.